★ Supreme Court ★

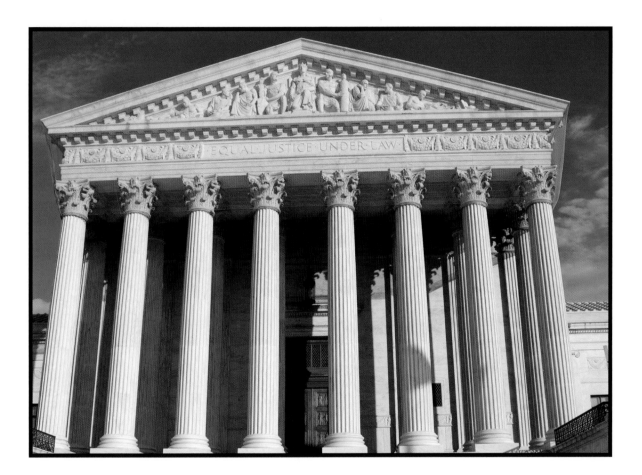

Katherine Krieg

rourkeeducationalmedia.com

Scan for Related Titles and Teacher Resources

Before Reading:

Building Academic Vocabulary and Background Knowledge

Before reading a book, it is important to tap into what your child or students already know about the topic. This will help them develop their vocabulary, increase their reading comprehension, and make connections across the curriculum.

1. *Look at the cover of the book. What will this book be about?*
2. *What do you already know about the topic?*
3. *Let's study the Table of Contents. What will you learn about in the book's chapters?*
4. *What would you like to learn about this topic? Do you think you might learn about it from this book? Why or why not?*
5. *Use a reading journal to write about your knowledge of this topic. Record what you already know about the topic and what you hope to learn about the topic.*
6. *Read the book.*
7. *In your reading journal, record what you learned about the topic and your response to the book.*
8. *After reading the book complete the activities below.*

Content Area Vocabulary
Read the list. What do these words mean?

appoints
argue
bench
interpret
interpretation
jury
rank
ruling
seniority
upheld
witnesses

After Reading:

Comprehension and Extension Activity

After reading the book, work on the following questions with your child or students in order to check their level of reading comprehension and content mastery.

1. *How is a Supreme Court hearing different from a regular court hearing? (Summarize)*
2. *Explain why there isn't a jury in the Supreme Court. (Infer)*
3. *How long do justices serve on the Supreme Court? (Summarize)*
4. *Of the 7,000 or more cases they have to choose from each year, which type of cases are the justices looking for? (Summarize)*
5. *Why do cases go to the Supreme Court? (Summarize)*

Extension Activity

Further research one of the cases from the book. What were the steps taken prior to going to the Supreme Court? Why did the case need to be heard by the Supreme Court? How did the issue come about? Were there any past issues or was this the first one? Were there any issues with beliefs, states' rights, or violence? Create a timeline that best represents your case and present it to your classmates.

Table of Contents

The Supreme Court of the United States has an important job.

The U.S. Constitution is a document that states the basic rights of U.S. citizens. It is the Supreme Court's job to make sure those rights are **upheld**.

More than 100 countries have used the U.S. Constitution as a model for their own.

Some people disagree about what certain parts of the Constitution mean. The Supreme Court must **interpret** the Constitution's meaning.

The Supreme Court was formed in 1790.

The Court receives about 7,000 petitions every year. It has almost complete control over which cases it will hear.

The Supreme Court is also known as the judicial branch of the government. The Court checks on the president and the U.S. Congress. It makes sure that neither is breaking the rules in the Constitution.

Three Branches of Government

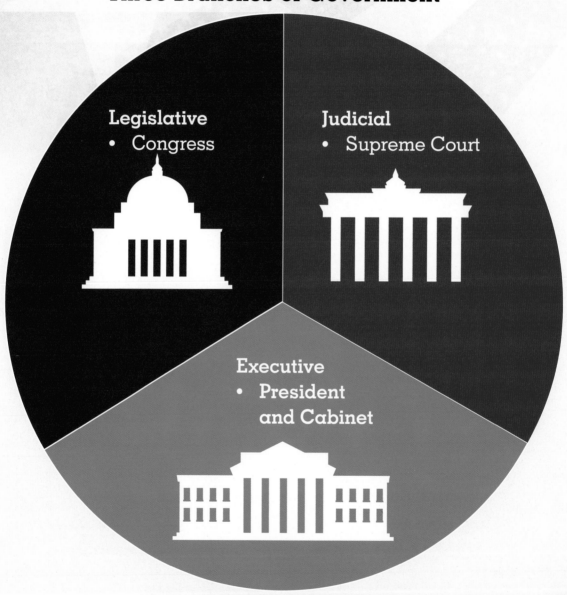

Legislative
• Congress

Judicial
• Supreme Court

Executive
• President and Cabinet

The Supreme Court is also known as the High Court or the Highest Court.

Throughout the United States, arguments can be handled in court. But in some court cases, the answer is not clear. These are the kinds of cases that might be heard by the Supreme Court.

The Supreme Court is made up of nine justices. One of these is the chief justice of the United States. The chief justice leads the other eight members of the Court.

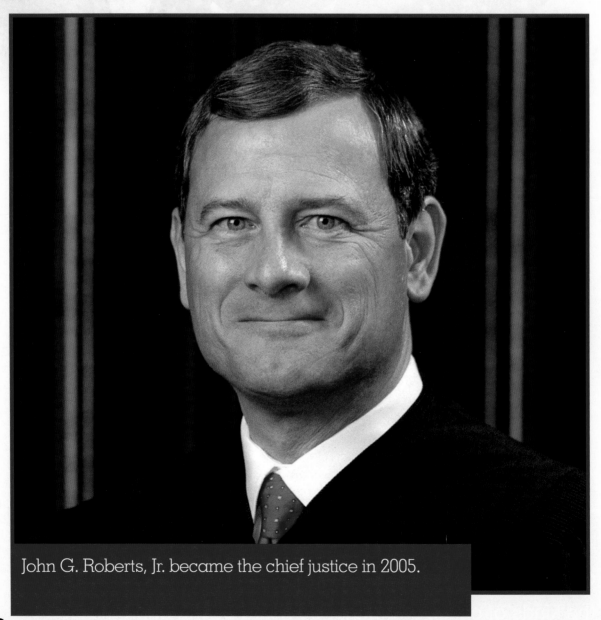

John G. Roberts, Jr. became the chief justice in 2005.

The president **appoints** the justices. Sometimes senators or members of the House of Representatives give the president an idea of who to pick. The president's choice must be confirmed by a Senate vote.

The other eight justices are sometimes called associate justices.

President Barack Obama appointed Sonia Sotomayor, left, to the Supreme Court in 2009.

The justices can serve in the Supreme Court for as long as they want. Most serve for about 16 years.

Associate Justice William O. Douglas (1898–1980) was the longest serving justice. He served for 36 years.

Antonin Scalia has been the longest-serving justice on the modern Supreme Court.

Most justices have a different **rank** based on how long they have been justices. They may have other small tasks based on their **seniority**.

The Supreme Court term starts on the first Monday in October. The day starts at 10:00 a.m. and ends around 3:00 p.m. The justices hear cases and make rulings until the term ends in June or July.

When the Court is called to order at the start of a day, the following statement is read: "Oyez! Oyez! Oyez! All persons having business before the honorable, the Supreme Court of the United States, are admonished to draw near and give their attention, for the Court is now sitting. God save the United States and this Honorable Court."

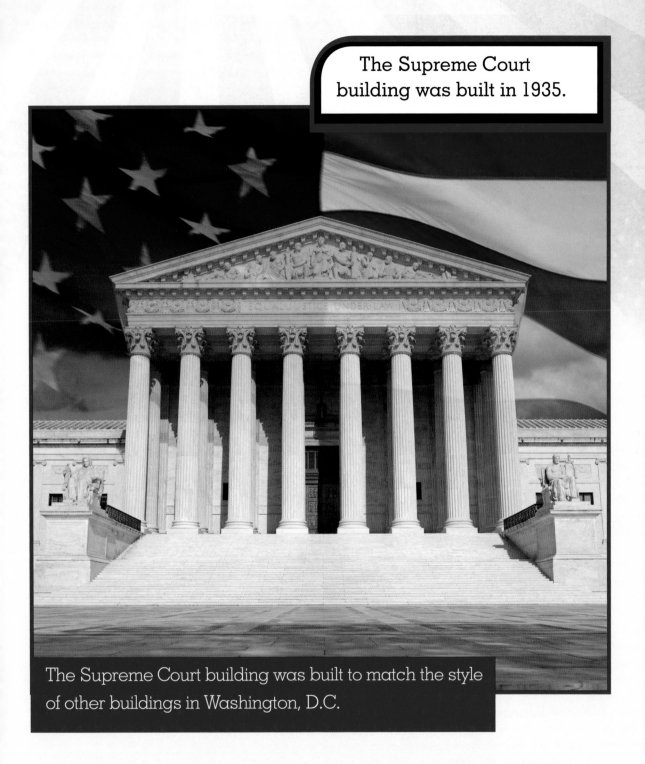

The Supreme Court
building was built in 1935.

The Supreme Court building was built to match the style of other buildings in Washington, D.C.

The Supreme Court meets in the Supreme Court building. It is in Washington, D.C. The justices sit on a **bench** raised off the floor. They wear black robes.

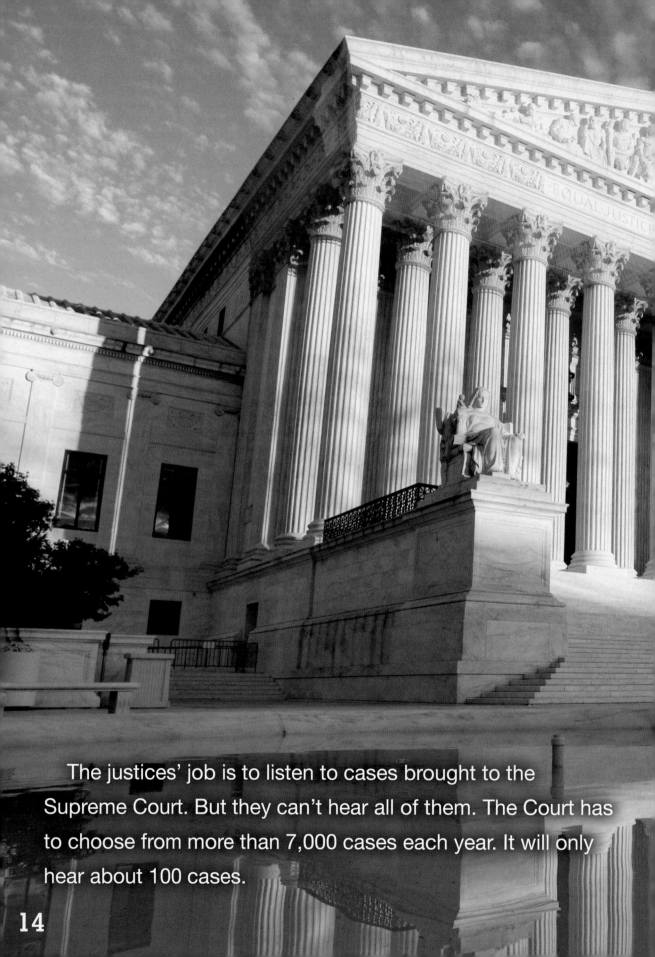

The justices' job is to listen to cases brought to the Supreme Court. But they can't hear all of them. The Court has to choose from more than 7,000 cases each year. It will only hear about 100 cases.

The justices pick cases that have to do with the **interpretation** of a law. They also hear cases about social issues. The justices vote to decide which cases they will hear. If at least four justices want to hear the case, it will be heard by the Court.

Hearing a Case

At a Supreme Court hearing, there are no **witnesses** as there are in most other courts. Instead, lawyers for each side **argue** their position.

Lawyers study and understand the laws in the United States.

When justices are hearing a case, it is called a sitting. When justices meet privately, it is called a recess.

After the Court makes a decision, all other courts in the United States must follow the Supreme Court's ruling.

After the justices have heard the arguments, they meet privately. They discuss the case, and then vote to make a decision.

In the Supreme Court, there is no **jury**. The justices make the **ruling** together. And, once the Court makes a decision on a case, it is final. The case cannot go to any other court.

Through the years, the Supreme Court has made important decisions that have changed the lives of Americans.

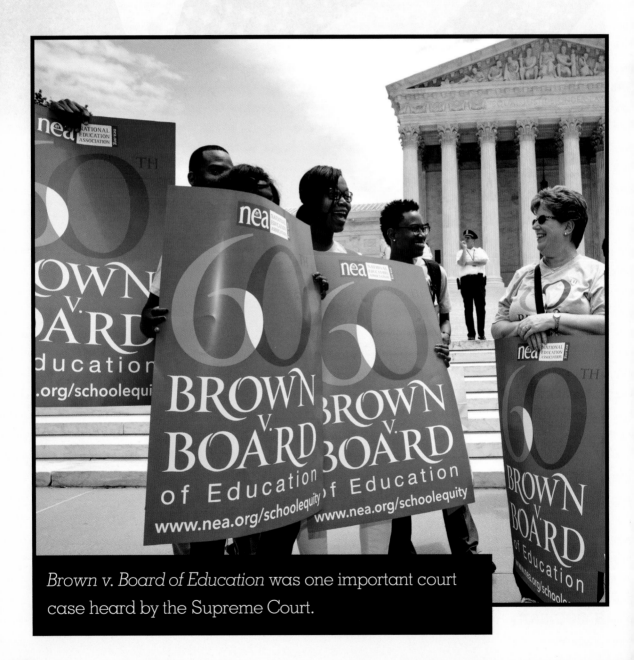

Brown v. Board of Education was one important court case heard by the Supreme Court.

Case Name	Details	Social Outcome	Date of Ruling
Plessy v. Ferguson	The Court ruled that racial segregation was constitutional.	Racial segregation continued in the United States.	May 18, 1896
Brown v. Board of Education	The Court ruled that the separation of black and white students in public schools was unconstitutional.	U.S. public schools were desegregated.	May 17, 1954
Roe v. Wade	The Court ruled that under the constitutional right to privacy a woman should be able to choose to have an abortion.	Abortion remained legal in the United States.	January 22, 1973
United States v. Windsor	The Court ruled that the Defense of Marriage Act, which defined marriage as a union between one man and one woman, was unconstitutional.	Same-sex marriages were recognized by federal law, even if they were not recognized on the state-level.	June 26, 2013

The United States is full of many people from different backgrounds. Disagreements about laws will always happen.

The Supreme Court is there to be the final voice in these disagreements. The justices work hard to correctly interpret the Constitution and maintain fairness in the United States.

IT IS EMPHATICALLY THE PROVINCE AND DUTY OF THE JUDICIAL DEPARTMENT TO SAY WHAT THE LAW IS.

MARBURY v. MADISON

1803

This engraving on the first floor of the Supreme Court building reminds justices and visitors of the Court's purpose.

Glossary

appoints (uh-POINTS): to pick someone for a job

argue (ARH-gyoo): to explain reasons for the court to decide a certain way

bench (bench): the place where a judge sits in court

interpret (in-TUR-prit): to decide the meaning of something

interpretation (in-TUR-prit-ta-tion): someone's idea of what something means

jury (JOOR-ee): a group of people that listen to a court case and decide if an accused person is guilty or not

rank (rangk): a job's level

ruling (ROO-ling): the decision made by a court

seniority (SEE-nyur-it-tee): having a higher rank

upheld (uhp-HEHLD): for a decision to be confirmed

witnesses (WIT-nis-is): people who give evidence in a court

Index

Show What You Know

1. How many justices make up the Supreme Court?
2. Who selects the justices?
3. How do justices decide which cases they will hear?
4. How might a Supreme Court decision affect your life?
5. Why do you think the founding fathers wanted a Supreme Court?

Websites to Visit

www.congressforkids.net/Judicialbranch_supremecourt.htm
www.socialstudiesforkids.com/subjects/supremecourt.htm
bensguide.gpo.gov/3-5/government/national/scourt.html

About the Author

Katherine Krieg is an author of many books for young people. Katherine enjoys following the results of U.S. Supreme Court cases in the news.

Meet The Author!
www.meetREMauthors.com

www.rourkeeducationalmedia.com

PHOTO CREDITS: Cover/Title Page © mdgn; page 4 © Onur Ersin; page 5 © Mark Wilson; page 6 © iconeer; page 7 © Moodboard; page 8 © Steve Petteway; page 9 © Pete Souza; page 10, 12 © Library of Congress; page 11 © AP Images/Pablo Martinez Monsivals; page 13, 14 © Gary Blakeley; page 16 © Stephen Coburn; page 17 © ikiryo; page 18 © AP Images; page 20 © swatjester; page 21 © Mesut Dogan

Edited by: Jill Sherman

Cover by: Nicola Stratford, nicolastratford.com
Interior design by: Jen Thomas

Library of Congress PCN Data

Supreme Court/ Katherine Krieg
 (U.S. Government and Civics)
  ISBN 978-1-62717-680-4 (hard cover)
  ISBN 978-1-62717-802-0 (soft cover)
  ISBN 978-1-62717-918-8 (e-Book)
Library of Congress Control Number: 2014935455

Printed in the United States of America, North Mankato, Minnesota

Also Available as:

ROURKE'S
e-Books